JOE WHITE

Joe White is an award-winning writer from Birmingham who makes work for stage, screen and audio. He was a previous member of the Old Vic 12 and BBC Drama Writers' Programme, and was the recipient of the Royal Literary Fund's J.B. Priestley Award for Writers of Promise and the Channel 4 Playwriting Award. His debut play *Mayfly* opened at the Orange Tree Theatre in spring 2018 to critical acclaim, leading to a nomination for Best Writer at The Stage Debut Awards, and winning the OffWestEnd Award for Most Promising New Playwright.

Other Titles in this Series

Joe White

BLACKOUT SONGS

NICK HERN BOOKS

London
www.nickhernbooks.co.uk

A Nick Hern Book

Blackout Songs first published in Great Britain in 2022 as a paperback original by Nick Hern Books Limited, The Glasshouse, 49 Goldhawk Road, London W12 8QP

Blackout Songs copyright © 2022 Joe White

Joe White has asserted his moral right to be identified as the author of this work

Cover image: PhotoAlto Images/Marin via Mediabakery

Designed and typeset by Nick Hern Books, London
Printed in the UK by Mimeo Ltd, Huntingdon, Cambridgeshire PE29 6XX

A CIP catalogue record for this book is available from the British Library

ISBN 978 1 83904 139 6

Blackout Songs was first performed at Hampstead Theatre Downstairs, London, on 4 November 2022. The cast was as follows:

HIM	Alex Austin
HER	Rebecca Humphries

Director	Guy Jones
Designer	Anisha Fields
Lighting	Christopher Nairne
Sound	Holly Khan
Movement	Iskandar R. Sharazuddin

Acknowledgements

I'd like to thank Joe Walker, Michael Kopelman and all the members of Alcoholics Anonymous who gave me their time and their stories while researching this play – it wouldn't be what it is without you. I owe nearly everything to Guy Jones for encouraging me to be braver, though less so for making me go on loads of walks. To Anisha, Kit, Holly, Iskandar, Isobel and Ciara for making the room such a joy and the piece so beautiful. To Roxana Silbert, Greg Ripley-Duggan, Tessa Walker and everyone at Hampstead Theatre – thank you for championing this play, particularly in such difficult times. To Pats and Harry for helping me see it for the first time, and to Simon, Tim and Katie, always, for keeping me going. A massive thank you to my agent, Howard Gooding, and everyone at Nick Hern Books, as well as the Peggy Ramsay Foundation and the Royal Literary Fund – I wouldn't still be writing if it wasn't for your help. And eternal thank yous to Alex Austin and Rebecca Humphries for making it better than I could ever imagine – I'll carry it forever.

J.W.

For Mum and Dad, always

Characters

HIM
HER

Note on Text

/ indicates the point of overlapping dialogue.

– at the end of a line indicates an interruption. One in the middle of a line is a shift in thought, or a change in tack.

(Dialogue in brackets is not quite said out loud.)

A space in-between dialogue marks an unknown gap in time – a blackout in memory.

NB: They should never be played drunk, but when alcohol is in their system they should oscillate at a higher frequency – as if they were capable of doing anything. Also, the marked stammers for Him are only a suggestion and I encourage the actor to find their own rhythm.

This text went to press before the end of rehearsals and so may differ slightly from the play as performed.

He wears a neck brace. She wears sunglasses. They stare at each other for a while.

HER. My round.

HIM. ...hm?

HER. My – The – Thing – It's a joke – The coffee thing. Urn.

HIM. oh –

HER. Vat, it's a vat, really, they should just hook us all up, shouldn't they, are you having one?

HIM. n-no –

HER. Just standing here then.

HIM. y-yeah.

HER. Is it okay if I stand with you?

HIM. (Of course.)

HER. Thank you. Thanks.

Coffee coffee coffee.

Fucking dreadful, aren't they.

HIM. Hm?

She indicates the room.

HER. Or are they friends of yours?

HIM. N-no. F-first time –

HER. First time, me too, first time for me too, what happened to your neck?

HIM. O-oh. I d-d-don't remember.

HER.…Right… And is the stammer. Related?

HIM. Uh…

HER. I think it's (attractive) … I knew a man with a stammer
once. He died in prison. Never got to finish his sentence.

Beat.

Sorry, that was – I'm nervous.

HIM. I-it's okay.

Pause.

HER. I was forced to come, you see. Under duress, practically,
practically at gunpoint, he's waiting for me across the –
The George and Dragon. Of all the fucking (places) – I'm
like a dog he's tied outside the butcher's. And, I mean, he
just – he just wants to say he tried, really, it's not like he
actually – It's the talking bit I'm nervous about – actually
loves me – And it's not like I'm bad at talking, I'm good at
talking, you can see that –

HIM. Y-yes –

HER. But it's not the type of talking they want, is it. They want
talking, don't they.

HIM. N-never been here before –

HER. I never remember anything, that's my problem. The
things they want me to remember anyway, if it's of no use to
me, it's gone. Take this for example. Here. Look. I found
this, this morning, in my coat pocket. You see that?

Nothing there.

HIM. Mm.

HER. It's a tooth.

HIM. I s-see it.

HER. It's not mine.

HIM. o-okay –

HER. You must understand – I don't go around collecting
    people's / teeth.

HIM. I w-wasn't –

HER. I'm just saying it was there, that's all I'm saying. And
    some people might (panic), you know, but my brain, my
    brain's just gone 'pfff, don't worry about it'. Gone. And
    that's – Well, that's what, exactly? That's *mercy*, isn't it?
    This is what mercy looks like, people could only dream of
    having a brain like – do you know you're shaking?

HIM. Wh-what?

HER. Shaking – Your hand.

HIM. O-oh.

HER. Are you okay?

HIM. Y-yeah – Uh, yes, yeah –

HER. You don't look okay.

HIM. I-I – I w-was a b-bit s-sick.

HER. What's that?

HIM. I-I was sick.

HER. Sick?

HIM. In a bin, o-out –

HER. Wait, you didn't – You didn't just stop, did you?

HIM. Wh-what?

HER. You didn't just stop, today? This morning, you didn't just
    stop –

HIM. Uh…

HER. Oh no, darling. Oh no, you can't do that, my love, you
    can't just stop, that's very bad, that's dangerous, you know
    it's one in twenty?

HIM. O-one in –

HER. Are you hallucinating or anything?

HIM. H-hallu/cinating?

HER. Spiders, usually. Spiders or rats, it tends to – You're quite
    clammy, you know that? Are you a clammy person normally?

HIM. N-no.

HER. Because you're quite clammy now.

HIM (*wanting to slow down*). S-sorry –

HER (*looking around for an exit*). So, yeah, so I'm just
    wondering –

HIM. S-sorry, o-o-one in t-   twenty, w-what?

HER. What?

HIM. Y-you s-said o-one in t-   twenty.

HER. Yes.

HIM. W-what?

HER. Die.

HIM. *D-   die?*

HER. But don't worry, it won't be you, my darling, I'm going
    to take care of you.

HIM. f-fuck –

HER. I descend from a long line of survivors, I know all the
    tricks. You need a bit of medicine is all. Straighten you out.
    And I'll join you. I feel a bit sick myself, all this fucking
    coffee – Just walk with me out here, don't look at them, just
    walk, calmly, normally, is that how you normally walk?

HIM. They're a-about / to s-start –

HER. Just popping out for some fresh –

    thank fuck for that, fucking people, Jesus, day of the living
    dead – ·

HIM. Wh-what about your... In the p-pub?

HER. Oh, no, fuck him, he'll have forgotten me anyway. Right, before we go spending our allowance, have you got anything at yours?

HIM. A-anything.

HER. Medicine. Where do you live?

HIM. Oh, uh, this, uh, sh-shared, uh – sh-shared –

HER. Shared –

HIM. Studio – w-warehouse, s-sort of –

HER. Squat.

HIM. What? N-no –

HER. You pay anything? To share this studio, warehouse –

HIM. Uh... w-well –

HER. Then that's a squat, you squat, you're a squatter, it's okay, leave it to me, I can call in a few favours, what's the time?

HIM. Uh –

HER. It will be fine, I know a place, I know the secret knock.

  just up here

HIM. Uh-huh.

HER. Dylan Thomas used to come here. Freud too. The painter, not the slip. I made a Freudian slip the other day. I was having breakfast with my husband, and I meant to say: 'darling, could you please pass the *milk*'... but what actually came out was: 'you fucking cunt you've ruined my life'. That was a joke.

HIM. O-oh.

HER. I'm not married, don't / panic –

HIM. A-actually c-can w-we s-stop a / s-second –

HER. okay, what's happening here.

HIM. I j-just I j-just –

HER. Just breathe, you're alright –

HIM. I j-just – I j-just don't know if this is a g-good idea,
a-actually –

HER. A good idea, what, saving your life?

HIM. I just – I just – I just, I know what I'm – I kn-know what
I *d-do* wh-when I –

HER. What you do?

HIM. I ch-   change. I change. D-do s-stupid, d-dangerous
things. D-don't r-recognise… A-and th-this was m-my
l-last chance, s-   so –

HER. Last chance?

HIM. Mm –

HER. With whom, with your girlfriend? Or, or boyfriend,
I don't –

HIM. N-no – M-m   my college.

HER. Your –

Your college? You go to – / You're telling me I'm trying to
shag a teenager –

HIM. N-no. A-art college – What?

HER. What?

HIM. S-say shag?

HER. I don't think so –

HIM. My art college said I h-had t-to s-stop…

HER. Oh, for fuck's sake, is nothing sacred any more? Now
they're coming for the artists, I mean, who's next, the
writers? Imagine if someone told – told *Bacon* to dry out?
Or – Or Van Gogh – Anyway, look, it's only *one* we're
talking about here. A *sip*, really, a tiny *whiff* of medicine,
level you out, save your life. You can't possibly let me spend

the rest of my life wondering if that gorgeous boy from that thing went out and died, now come on, I'll hold your hand if you like. There. Alright?

HIM. Alright.

HER. Now do you want to do a quick eulogy, before we –

HIM. Eu-eulogy –

HER. I don't do goodbyes you see.

HIM. I-I'm okay.

HER. Oh, come on now, there must be something you're going to miss about it.

HIM. L-like what?

HER. Well, I don't know, I've been drinking since I was twelve, darling, I've never missed it.

HIM. T-twelve.

HER. From my first sip, I knew, I was (hooked).

HIM. I d-don't th-think I'll m-miss anything. I hate it.

HER. You hate it? Then why are you in trouble with it?

HIM. B-because it w-works. I-it m-makes me… f-feel better. F-for a bit.

Th-the l-lightness. B-back of my head.

HER. Back of your –

HIM. L-like. S-someone holding it? S-someone's f-fingers in my hair. Th-that's what I always… S-someone, s-stroking my h-head…

She touches the back of his head. She puts her hand through his hair.

HER. Like that? Feels like that?

HIM. A-a bit.

HER. But not quite.

HIM. N-no.

HER. Now that's our eulogy. 'Not quite. Nothing quite.'

Oh well. To the last one ever. Cheers.

HIM. Ch-cheers.

God blows through the room

His neck brace is gone. He stares at her. A while.

Have you got my tooth?

I was told you might… In your pocket, maybe…

Pause.

I'm – Okay, I think this has backfired –

HER. Why would I / have your tooth?

HIM. When we met you / had a tooth.

HER. We've met?

HIM. Ha. Yeah – what? *Yes* – Are you…

We came here, and we had. Medicine. I was. Shaking –
Wow, nothing, really, okay / fuck me –

HER. Yeah, *wow*, I was having a / drink, actually so, fucking
wow yourself – *Wow* –

HIM. This is the best acting I've seen in – / Fucking, round of
applause over here –

HER. Sorry – Act– Who's acting – who the fuck is acting?

HIM. You could just be polite and let me down gently you
know –

HER. Let you down – I don't have a fucking clue who you are –

HIM. Well then that's worse, then, if that's true, that's scary,
     that's actually quite / fucking –

HER. Scary?

HIM. You should be scared, yeah –

HER. Because I forgot you?

HIM. Cos you forgot the night we had. It was a great night.

HER. Well, clearly not.

HIM. Yeah, no, you're right, so I'll just go and jump in the
     fucking Thames then, shall I? Nice knowing you –

HER. You wore a neck brace.

   Beat.

HIM. What?

HER. There was a – You wore a neck brace. And-and a
     stammer? You stammered.

HIM. No.

HER. Yes, you did.

HIM. Sorry, can you – can – Can you hear a stammer?

HER. Well yes / actually –

HIM. Yeah, well, just then I did, but I – I think I'd remember if
     I had a fucking neck brace on –

HER. Well, where's that come from then?

HIM. I have no idea, some other conquest obviously –

HER. Were you this fantastic to look at before?

HIM. Wh-what?

HER. You can't have been, I'd have remembered. How do I look?

HIM. Uh…

HER. Oh, that bad, really –

HIM. No, no, good, you look –

HER. Oh Christ, no I don't, stop it –

HIM. You look great.

HER. You stammered when you came.

HIM. What?

HER. That's why – I was like, why's that lodged there – You
were like. O-o-oh f-f-f-fuck, I remember now, don't worry, it
was fine, probably, and who cares, I went with someone
once, every time we had sex he was like 'get ready', that's
all he'd say 'get ready, get ready, get ready'. And I was like
for what? To this day I don't know what he thought was on
its way –

HIM. Well, we didn't actually.

HER. We didn't? You said we had a great night?

HIM. Yeah, but we / didn't –

HER. So, what was so great about it then?

HIM. You know what –

HER. No, I'm serious – I seriously want to remember.

HIM (*showing his arm. Nothing there*). How about that, you
remember that?

HER. What am I looking at here, your arm –

HIM. My scar, here. Cut it on the window.

HER. Window?

HIM. We broke a window.

HER. Yeah, you've got the wrong person –

HIM. Window at my college, you threw / something and –

HER. Sorry, college? / You're telling me I tried to shag a
teenager –

HIM. A-art college. Yeah, you said that / before – You wanted
to see one of my paintings –

HER. Art college. Wait, that sounds – You're an artist, yes.

HIM. So we broke into the college, and – It-it was this big oil thing? On canvas. All these, like, limbs?

HER. Limbs? Limbs you say.

HIM. Limbs, yeah, in oil, big, abstract, kind of – Anyway, that's not – the painting's not the – We were looking at it. And, you know, my arm was fucking – and we were stood, and the moon through the window was… big – What am I doing – this / is fucking stupid –

HER. No, no it's not, please, carry on I want to remember. Please. We were looking at your painting of limbs, and… the moon was really big and…

HIM. We stood there… This amazing light… And you got closer to me, and you said, you said. Something. Something, about remembering me. In this perfect light… And then we… kissed, and… Nearly two years at that college, and that was the closest I've felt to… Anything…

Beat.

HER. Are you sure this wasn't someone else –

HIM. Oh yeah actually now you say it, it wasn't you.

HER. Really –

HIM. No for fuck's sake. I've been looking for you since I got kicked out.

Beat.

HER. Looking / for me?

HIM. Yeah, I realise that sounded a bit weird –

HER. Looking for *me*. / *Looking* for me –

HIM. Not in a – Not like that –

HER. Out for revenge, or something, out for blood, on the hunt.

HIM. I just wanted more. I just wanted more…

Beat.

HER....Can we start again? Is that possible, do you think?
I mean, that's the mercy of all this, isn't it, slates wiped. What
if I just walked up to you now – You, just standing there –

HIM. It's okay, we don't have to / do –

HER. Hello –

HIM. right we're doing it –

HER. Is it okay if I stand with you?

HIM. Yeah, sure.

HER. You come here often?

HIM. First time.

HER. First time, yes, not for me. It's my favourite bolt-hole.
Whole city. Dylan Thomas drank here. We're in the centre of
the triangle. The French, Coach and Colony. It's just like the
Bermuda one – people go missing here too.

HIM. Right –

HER. I'm Agatha.

HIM. Agatha.

HER. Tabatha. Tabatha Thomas, distant relative, also a poet,
doomed, of course, I'll never live up to the name, so I just
I sit in here all day, haunted, hunted, *missing*... I live nearby.
Little bedsit, off Dean, above a sex shop, inherited, of
course, all dust and furs and taxidermy, moaning downstairs,
I completely adore it – I missed your name...

HIM. Oh, uh... Derrick.

HER. Derrick...

HIM. Yeah –

HER. And what do you do, Derrick?

HIM. I. Uh. I weld. I'm a welder.

HER....Oh...

HIM. Or or, something else –

HER. Something else I think –

HIM. Uh, well –

HER. Aren't you that singer? That famous singer, all the
    basement bars –

HIM. I don't think so –

HER. I think he's so sexy, that singer, I've always said I'd shag
    him rotten if I met him –

HIM. I'm the singer, yeah.

HER. I thought so.

HIM. I just tell people I weld cos I don't like the fame –

HER. Buy these drinks, won't you, Derrick.

HIM. I don't, uh… I wish I could, b-but I'm, I'm a bit strapped
    at the moment. I'm struggling… with my music, you see,
    i-inspiration –

HER. Well, then I tell you what, Derrick. I'll buy your drink if
    you sing me a song…

HIM. What?

HER. I've just come into some money, you see. My father's ill,
    apparently. *Gravely ill.*

HIM. Oh, sorry.

HER. No, not sorry, no, absent, narcissist, *actor* – and not a
    very good one either, not so much tour de force as forced to
    tour, you know, and anyway, he won't die. Oh no, he always
    does this. Every few years… Some people have an awful
    habit of living, don't you find?

HIM. Uh. No. Actually.

HER. Oh, well, I do. So how about you do me one of your hits,
    and I'll buy you a drink. I'll pay for your whole night.
    What's that one go like…

She starts to improvise a song. Maybe it's about a neck brace, or a missing tooth.

It's *your* song…

You want a drink, you have sing for it…

She carries on. Eventually he joins in – sings it at the same time, the same lyrics. A game. He gets carried away, gets louder, she laughs.

God blows through the room

She's looking in his mouth. It's full of blood. He can barely touch his lips together.

You must remember something –

HIM. Jus' woke up outside the 'u'.

He tries saying 'pub' again. It sounds a bit like 'hut'.

The 'u'…

HER. The pub.

HIM. Yeah.

HER. But, darling, I mean, was it – Were you in a fight? Did you – Did you fall?

HIM. I-I-I don't know. I don't…

He laughs a little bit. He thinks. It's all gone.

(*Upset.*) Fuck. I'm sorry, / fuck's sake.

HER. No, it's – Oh, don't – Don't say sorry –

HIM. Fucking stupid.

HER. I think it's sexy, actually. Desperately romantic. You're so *doomed* aren't you.

HIM. That's romantic?

HER. Oh, that's the only romance there is.

HIM. Is it really bad?

HER. Well, you've – Your tongue is all cut up, and you've –
I think you've chipped a few – There's quite a few… bits…
of teeth, in all the (blood) –

HIM. Fuck.

HER. And, I think this one – uh. This one at the back is, sort
of… split…

HIM. S'lit?

HER. You must have hit something quite hard. I think you need
to go to hospital –

Now, we can – Is it too late to get a bus or –

HIM. I I I can't do that –

HER. It's okay, I'll come with you –

HIM. I won't come back out.

HER. What? Of course you'll come back out, darling –

HIM. I won't. I won't –

HER. Your tooth is split in half –

HIM. I'M NOT FUCKING –

I'm not going to hospital – Sorry. Sorry. (*Upset.*) Sorry.
Fuck –

HER. It's okay –

HIM. You're so lovely.

HER. Alright –

HIM. I need you to do it.

HER. What?

HIM. I need you – I need you to 'ull it out.

HER. No you fucking do / not.

HIM. 'lease. It hurts so much – If I can j-just –

HER. I can't – How do you expect me / to even –

HIM. You've go' 'lyers, in your kitchen drawer.

He gestures plyers.

HER. *Plyers?*

HIM. Yeah –

HER. Right, yeah, no fucking chance, I'm sorry –

HIM. J-just quick –

HER. I can't – / I can't do that –

HIM. You can. Please. Can you –

Can you say some'hin'.

HER. What?

HIM. Distrac' me while you – Just tal'.

HER. You think I can talk *and* do this –

HIM. I thin' you can tal' through any'hing –

HER. What do you want me to talk about?

HIM. (I dunno.) First time we met.

HER. Oh Christ, I have no idea.

HIM. Anythin', for fuck's sake, it's doing my / head in –

HER. Okay. Okay… First time we met…

Uh. I remember… I remember a hut.

HIM. A wha'?

HER. Stop talking – There was this hut, a wooden hut. In a field. And I was inside it. On a little bed. Straw. And I had all these sores. Like skin sores all over me, I was sick, I had the plague. This is another life – you understand.

HIM. Oh.

HER. First time we met. You don't remember this? When I was in a hut with the plague?

HIM. I'm tryin'.

HER. So, I was there, and you were in the next, next *hamlet*, and you loved me very much, I'm just going to give this a little pull and see if –

HIM. FUCK –

HER. Okay, not just yet – So, so anyway, you loved me but I had the plague. And I told someone to tell you. I gave someone a note, to give to you, telling you to stay away from me, to go find someone else, live your life, but you, you couldn't understand, you were so, uh, so –

HIM. Illi'rate.

HER. Betrothed.

HIM. Ah.

HER. You were so *obsessed* with me, you couldn't resist, and so you came to me, in the night, and we hadn't consummated before God yet, I don't think, I'm feeling like no we didn't, just sort of… you know…

HIM. Wha's tha'?

HER. Lingering glances.

HIM. Oh.

HER. In the market square.

HIM. Okay.

HER. You sell potatoes. Lots of lingering glances –

HIM. I sell 'o'a'oes –

HER. And you came, to my hut, in the night –

HIM. I sell 'o'a'oes –

HER. You came in the night and you knocked upon my door –

HIM. 'upon'.

HER. Thrice upon, and I told you, through the wood – the wooden – uh, *slats* – I told you – I told you not to come here, you fool, you idiot, you'll die, but you said no, you're crying and –

HIM. Nay.

HER. What?

HIM. Would have said nay back then –

HER. What, like a horse? You're a man in / this reincarnation.

HIM. I know that – / Doesn't matter, just –

HER. Stop inter– This is my memory, okay – So you're outside my door, grazing fucking grass apparently, and I'm in my hut, going stay away, begone, flee, *live*, but you're like, *nay*, and you burst down the door, and take me in your arms, and I fling back, like that, and you say something amazing like, like, I'd rather die with you than –

HIM. There's no life without you.

HER. Yes, *yes*, oh my / God yes –

HIM. Look at you –

HER. So you're holding me –

HIM. You're amazing –

HER. and then you kiss me, even though I'm all plaguey and falling apart, and my lips are falling off –

HIM. I would / you know. Kiss you. I would –

HER. you kiss me and it's amazing, it's the best kiss in the world, and I melt into you, my whole body like absorbs. And you kiss me, and you drink me in, all of me, all my sickness and sores, all of it disappears into you, and I'm gone, I'm vanished, and you're alive, but you're also like going to die too, now, now you've taken in all that plague, all that poison… And so the last thing… the last thing I did… was kill you… Don't you think that happened? In a past life.

Now, this is going to hurt.

HIM. Fuck.

HER. What?

HIM. The door's fucking – / We'll try the back one.

HER. Wait, wait, where are we?

HIM. They leave one of them open, for tramps, at night.

HER. Sorry, can we just – Things are getting a bit fucking
   (blurry) –

HIM. Free wine. Remember?

HER. Free wine.

HIM. Yes.

HER. And this is what you meant?

HIM. Yeah.

HER. Right, because – Because I thought you meant like
   a party or something.

HIM. A party? No. Did I say a party?

HER. No.

HIM. Right.

HER. You didn't say a church though.

HIM. Didn't I?

HER. No.

HER. Right, well, yeah, I meant a church –

HER. So, you're saying – We're stealing communion / wine now?

HIM. Stealing – We're not steal– It's charity, this is charity –
   What? Why are you looking at me like / that –

HER. We're not here, are we? Are we really fucking here
   already? We're not these people already, are we?

HIM. What people.

HER. People who steal fucking wine from fucking churches –

HIM. You always buy the drinks, right?

HER. What?

HIM. I don't ever have any money, do I. I stay round yours all the time. You buy me dinner.

HER. I like doing that.

HIM. But have I done anything for you? Have I sold a single painting, in all this time? Have I even finished one?

HER. I – I (don't know) –

HIM. No, I haven't. You should know that, I haven't. Not even a single one, I fucking tore up the last one – So, so this is me giving something to you. If not the wine, then the story. Won't forget *this* will you. Full moon, holy wine, it's like a fucking song or something – You know the world is different under a full moon? People are. People fall in love. Cos it pulls liquid around, doesn't it. Tides and that. And there's liquid in us too. Blood and whatever else. Chemicals. The brain is the moistest organ in the body. Moon drunk is different.

HER. That doesn't make any fucking sense –

HIM. Keep your voice down, people are sleeping –

HER. Don't take too many, we don't need / too many –

HIM. Shut up, sh–

HER. Oh, this is bad, this is really bad –

HIM. Why, do you believe in God or something?

HER. What?

HIM. Oh my God, you believe in God –

HER. Shut up.

HIM. If you don't, then you won't mind me having a quick –

HER. What are you doing?

HIM. I need a piss.

HER. Stop it –

HIM. What do you care, if you don't believe in God –

HER. Okay, yes, I do, a bit, for fuck's sake –

HIM. Wow.

HER. Yes, wow, yes, what, you've never prayed?

HIM. No.

HER. Well, I have, I do. I went to a Catholic boarding school from six, okay, some things stick to you, no matter how hard you try to shake them off. I mean, look at you, for instance –

HIM. Six?

HER. Yes.

HIM. That's young.

HER. Don't do that, don't try to do that –

HIM. Do what?

HER. Understand things, deep-dive, don't fucking do that, because I loved it, actually, I had a great time, all the God stuff, I was obsessed. My first drink was communion. I was twelve. It turns into blood, in your mouth, you know, Jesus's blood. It's still wine in the chalice, but as soon as it's past your lips, once it's in your mouth – And *you* do that. *You* bring God back to life by drinking wine. I mean, I didn't stand a chance, really.

Beat.

HIM. Can you do it?

HER. What?

HIM. That thing. God's blood. To me.

HER. No.

HIM. Why not? You don't remember?

HER. No, I remember –

HIM. So then, come on, show me – I'll take it serious, I promise. I promise. What do I do? Please. I want it...

Beat.

HER. First you kneel.

HIM. Kneel. Kneel here?

He kneels.

HER. And then. You put your head down, but eyes up. Eyes up at me.

HIM. Like this.

HER. And I stand over you. And I say… I say…

Behold… The lamb of God… Who taketh away the sins of the earth… And before the blood, you take the… The…

She holds her thumb out.

This is my body… Which I give up to you…

He sucks her thumb.

He kisses her hand. Her palms. Her wrists. He stops and looks up at her.

HIM. You know we're just drinking buddies, don't you.

Pause.

HER. Yeah… Yes –

HIM. I'll only forget you. Eventually…

She pours wine into his mouth and over him.

God blows through the room

In the dark, he thrashes, reeling in pain.

He is painting – creating something horrific.

They stare at each other for a long time. Maybe he's covered in red.

Jesus.

HER. Hi.

HIM. What are you – What are you doing here / what fucking time –

HER. I work for census. We're going around the area, checking for anyone we might have missed.

HIM. Missed –

HER. People go missing all the time. This city. Bermuda Triangles all over.

HIM. Me go missing? Me?

HER. So, single, married, divorced?

HIM. Okay, I'm shutting the door now –

HER. This is definitely a squat by the way –

HIM. Sorry, do you know how fucking mad this is? I'm just checking that you know, because – Because I haven't seen you – Since *you* went missing. *You*. I haven't seen you in –

HER. I've been busy –

HIM. Busy? Right. Busy with what, I mean you don't work, so… Busy with someone else, you mean? Busy fucking someone else –

HER. My dad died. Busy with that.

   Pause.

HIM. Is this…

   Is that real? Or is this –

HER. It's very real, yes, he's very really dead. His liver, exploded, basically, hand grenade in him, finally fucking popped. He was always playing with the pin –

HIM. Right. Well. Sorry.

HER. Ah. Luck of the draw, isn't it. Some people survive, some people don't. Anyway, I'm here to collect a debt.

HIM. A debt?

HER. I came with you to the pub once. Saved your life. You remember that? Now I need you to come somewhere with me.

HIM. Where?

HER. His funeral… Soon.

HIM. I'm sorry, it's just – This is – The last time I saw you, you told me we were just drinking buddies, and now / you want me to come –

HER. Wait a second, wait a second – *You* said that. You said 'drinking buddies' –

HIM. What the fuck, / no I didn't.

HER. That was you –

HIM. Why would I say that? Why the fuck would I have said that to you, do you know how much that hurt me? That really fucking hurt me. I went off the deep end after that. I went right off it. I did some stupid – Fucking dangerous things.

Beat.

HER. You've been painting though.

HIM. What?

HER. You look like you've been painting. There's red in your –

She goes to touch the back of his head, he dodges.

HIM. Yeah. Yes. I have.

HER. Well then. You're welcome. I should take commission.

I was in a pub, when I found out. Someone was talking about him. Some old man said my father's name, and then I heard him say. He went to hospital and never came out. That's how I heard my dad was dead. And I looked around the room, and I didn't know anyone, and no one knew me. I was no one. And then I thought – I remembered. Well, hang on. There is someone, isn't there. Someone knows me, in this city. Knows my smell, has kissed my neck. Who was that? Who was that person?

HIM. That was nice.

Nice service. If that means anything.

HER. Not really – What are those?

HIM. Flowers.

HER. They're dead.

HIM. Are they? No. Just need a bit of water –

HER. Where did you get them?

HIM. I bought them. Before – I left them –

HER. With what?

HIM. What?

HER. Bought with what, you haven't got any fucking…

   '*Dearest Gemima…* / *Forever in our hearts.*'

HIM. Oh there's a – Hang on –

HER. There's a note here, yeah –

HIM. Right, I didn't see that –

HER. So this was off someone else's –

HIM. Yeah.

HER. Grave.

HIM. Yeah. Fuck. (*Laughing.*) Fuck.

   I mean. Kind of funny. Gemima. Sorry, fuck. Sorry…

   He sounded like a character. Some of those stories. That one
   about him stealing the wine. Priest looked like he was going
   have a heart attack… I see where you get it –

HER. Doesn't mean anything, does it. Little slab. Little slab
   with your name on it, like you're special now, like most of
   the world isn't dead. What was it he kept saying? *We honour
   the memory…* I mean, what the fuck does that mean? *Whose*
   memory? Mine? I barely knew him. How am I supposed to
   honour the memory of someone I hardly remember? This is
   the most present he's ever been – Dad, slab, yeah, there you
   fucking are.

HIM. D-do you want to go get a / drink –

HER. I had this word… during the (service) – Going round –
    It's like… Ob… something. Ob…? Not ob*scure*.

HIM. Ob-ituary?

HER. No, no –

HIM. Obituary would make / sense –

HER. If you say obituary again, you'll be in a hole yourself –

HIM. Alright –

HER. Obscene.

HIM. What? Obscene.

HER. Yeah, obscene, yeah. Obscene. He used to talk about that
    word. The meaning – One of his little party tricks, round the
    dinner table, 'everyone listen to me, aren't I clever'. It comes
    from Greek, Greek plays. Means *offstage*. For all those
    things, you know. Terrible things. Someone's eyes being
    pulled out, shagging your mum, things we can't look at.
    The most we can manage is… someone standing there, some
    messenger, some old man in a pub saying *he's dead*. That
    character in your – That man, that unseen, obscene man, at
    the very edge of your life, well he's dead, he died, and you'll
    never really know him now because he's gone forever, and
    that's that. It's obscene. Whole thing.

    Pause.

HIM. Not forever.

HER. What?

HIM. Not forever, he's not… Not forever.

HER. What, so he's just having a lie-down is he?

HIM. No, but… You'll see him.

HER. Jesus Christ –

HIM. I'm not talking about… I mean – I'm talking about. Just,
    like. You'll be reminded of – We carry people, don't we.

Important people. We carry everyone we've ever loved, right on our backs, you know?

HER. No, I don't know, actually, I have no idea what the fuck you're / talking about –

HIM. Like my parents, right, I carry my parents, even if I don't want to –

HER. Are your parents dead?

HIM. Are they – Uh, no. No, I don't think so –

HER. Right, and have you ever lost anyone, ever, or are you just / saying stuff you've heard in –

HIM. Loads, yeah, I don't want / to fight –

HER. Loads. You're twelve years old. *Loads.*

HIM. All my best mates.

HER. What?

HIM. Doesn't matter – I told you this before – I don't want to fight –

HER. No, what, what are you talking about?

HIM. I was in hospital? When I was a kid. You remember this? I had cancer for like – Like my whole – I did school, there. It's where I started painting. All my mates were there, and a lot of them died, and I carry them, still. I have to try to remember, sometimes, to really try, but – He would have carried you, you know, he would have thought a lot about you –

HER. He sent me away when I was six, so, no, actually I don't think he did *carry me* –

HIM. Don't you think you're memorable?

Is that what you think – Cos he – Cos he sent you away, that means he tried to forget you?

HER. Okay, alright, thanks Dr Freud but I'm done here – Let's go get a fucking / drink –

HIM. You're the most memorable person I've ever met.

I-I mean it… Even – Even all them fucking old bastards we
meet, even the ones who forget their own names, even they
remember you. Even me. With my sieve of a head, when you
disappeared, I still saw you. All the time, bits of you. Your
eyes when you tell a story. Mole on your stomach. Touching
the back of my head… This is what happens when you love
someone. You keep them. Bits of them, you keep bits of
them with you all the time. Carry them. Little bits.

Pause.

HER. This is the first time you say it.

HIM. Yeah.

HER. *Here. Now* –

HIM. Yes –

HER. Could you see how that's a bit – How I'm in quite a
vulnerable fucking place here / and –

HIM. It just came out / I didn't mean it –

HER. I didn't say it back. Did you notice that?

HIM. I didn't say it for you to say it back –

HER. You can't buy me a drink today, but you can fucking say
that to me –

HIM. Yeah –

HER. I think I'd prefer the drink.

HIM. Well then. Let me – Let me find something. I know a
place. Free wine.

HER. Free wine?

HIM. Yeah.

HER. We've done that already.

HIM. Have we?

HER. I'm not doing that again.

She pours a bottle of wine on the ground.

There was this other time – oh God when was this – when
I got something published in a magazine and he'd read it –

HIM. Wait – You – You wrote something?

HER. Just – just a little poem, nothing – Calm down, it was
fairly awful –

HIM. It was published in a magazine, it can't have been / awful –

HER. I'm trying to tell you about my dad –

HIM. Sorry, sorry, just, wow –

HER. Yes wow, so it was this poem about me being like him, and
he'd read it, apparently, amazingly, and had this – I suppose he
had some guilt, all of a – latent, Catholic – because he said
he'd take me to a meeting. That we'd *both* go, and try
together, and I thought, I remember thinking maybe, really,
maybe this time, and we walked up to the – It was this church
hall, and we got to the door, he said, 'right then… here you
are'. And he crossed the road. To this pub, to The George
and – And that was maybe – Maybe that was the last time
I saw him, I don't know, really, I can't… You know, I wish
I could just… All of him – Just… (Wipe it all away.)

HIM. You don't mean that.

HER. Oh no, I do. I do. I wish I could wipe all of this. If I could
control my brain I would. I'm done with all of it. Aren't you?
Aren't you done? I'm serious, this could be it, couldn't it.
Last sip. Could be. If we wanted. Don't you think?

HIM. We?

HER. Yes.

HIM. We? Meaning, like, 'we'?

HER. I'm saying 'we', yes, I'm saying together, we do it
together

HIM. As a…

HER. Yes.

HIM. Couple.

HER. Yes. What do you think?

HIM. I think yes please.

HER. Yes, please.

HIM. Where do we start?

HER. Cupboards. Anything you find. My hiding places.

HIM. Hiding places?

HER. I tend to – I leave bottles for my – Around the flat.
    Sometimes – Little presents to my future self. I hardly ever
    remember where.

HIM. So we just look –

HER. Look, yes, bin bags. It will be like an Easter-egg hunt.

HIM. Most bottles wins.

HER. I know there's one in my underwear drawer. Under a
    jumper my dad gave me. Bin that too.

HIM. Got one. In a cupboard. By the boiler.

HER. One under the bed. Two of them under the bed –

HIM. Shelf, here –

HER. Under the kitchen sink. Next to the bleach.

HIM. Clinking. Like bells.

HER. Like a call to prayer.

HIM. What now?

HER. We pour them away. Just pour. Don't even smell it. Hold
    your breath and pour –

HIM. How much is this all together, do you think? A bath tub?

HER. A river, I don't know.

HIM. A river, yeah, fuck. I wonder how much we've swallowed, our entire lives. Rivers. Lakes. You know we swallow half a pint of each other's spit every time we have sex?

HER. What?

HIM. About that, yeah, depends how long, how much kissing –

HER. That's completely revolting.

HIM. What's that over years, do you think? If we had sex once a week, on average. Twenty-six pints a year. Let's say ten years. Maybe three hundred pints of spit –

HER. Fuck's sake, can you stop please? Ten years, Jesus.

HIM. Don't give us that long then?

HER. I don't give anything that long. Not even drinking your spit. Now pour.

This is good. This is good, isn't it? It's good.

HIM. It's good yeah.

HER. Can you see that?

HIM. Uh, what am I –

HER. Says 'misuse', see?

HIM. Right.

HER. The poster, there. *Alcohol misuse*. I mean how fucking ridiculous is that? That's not me is it. I know exactly how to fucking use it, I never misused it my entire life –

HIM. It's a phrase.

HER. How long, do you think?

HIM. A couple of minutes maybe – Are you okay?

HER. Just – Yes, just – Why are the lights in these buildings always so – Why are they so desperate to see us? Or for us to see each other? Fucking dreadful, the lot of them –

HIM. I'm here.

HER. What?

HIM. I'm just saying – Hold my hand a second –

HER. It's clammy.

HIM. Well, I'm nervous too.

HER. I'm not nervous, I'm fine, it's just the waiting – so much milling about, so much bloody coffee –

I'm not talking, you know. When they ask – I'm not talking about anything –

HIM. You don't have to talk about / anything –

HER. You do, look, he's standing up –

HIM. Sh –

HER. I mean, who wants to listen to all this? Why hold on to all this, when we can so easily –

Fucking tears now –

HIM. Sh –

HER. I mean, fucking hell, just forget it, try to forget it all, that's the fucking mercy of – What are you doing?

HIM. I'm going to talk –

HER. What?

HIM. It's okay, I'm just –

HER. No, no, don't do that.

HIM. I want to –

HER. What are you going to say?

HIM. I don't know – Just – Just talk about myself a bit.

HER. And me? You're going to talk about me too.

HIM. No.

HER. Of course you are, we're here together, aren't we, we're joined at the – we're practically the same fucking person –

HIM. No, we're not, just calm down –

HER. I don't – / I'm sorry I don't think I can actually –

HIM. Where are you – What are / you doing?

HER. You can do it, you can do it, I just – I need some fresh air –

HIM. You're shaking.

HER. No I'm not. Yes, I am. Fresh air. It was cold out.

HIM. Walking.

HER. Yes, walking, yeah, went for a walk.

HIM. Late.

HER. I like walking late. Nights like this. People out. What are you doing?

HIM. Kissing you –

HER. Don't – Don't do that –

HIM. What?

HER. Don't just come up and –

HIM. Okay –

HER. Sorry, I just – I just don't like it when you come up to my face like that, like a big dog.

HIM. Like a big dog.

HER. I wasn't ready is all. Let me have a mint. Let me –

Right. There. Minty fresh and ready. What? What's this look you're giving me – What? Do you want a blowjob? Minty fresh –

HIM. Did you drink today?

I'm sorry, I didn't – I shouldn't have said it like –

HER. Wow.

HIM. It's – It's okay if you did. We're in this together, right –

HER. I went out walking.

HIM. For five hours, at night, in Soho, in the cold –

HER. I needed to get out of this flat –

HIM. And not wanting to kiss me because –

HER. Because I find you repulsive. Right now, I find you completely and utterly. I didn't want to kiss you the second I got in, and now, what, now your ego, your ego is a little bruised and / you're saying all –

HIM. Alright – Sorry –

HER. You're accusing me of – Do you know how fucking awful that is? Saying we're in it together / and then –

HIM. I'm sorry, I'm – Fuck – Look, you know I'm proud of you –

HER. You're proud of me?

HIM. Yes. Yes. You're doing great, you're doing so well. I'm so proud of you.

HER. What is it?

HIM. What? Just open it.

HER. You know I don't like surprises, I never pull the right / expression –

HIM. Jesus, just unwrap the bloody thing, will you –

HER. I'd rather you just told me what it was instead / of all this charade –

HIM. Christ, have you never just opened a present?

HER. I hate presents, I always have, they always let you down.

HIM. Well not this one.

HER. This being?

HIM. Jesus.

HER. Just fucking tell me.

HIM. It's a book. Okay. It's a book for you to write in. For you to write poems in, or…

I thought maybe – I had a daydream the other day – I let my ego get the better of me – that you wrote a poem about me and it made you famous –

HER. fucking hell –

HIM. Someone said once that every man has two deaths. One, when he's buried in the ground. And the other is the last time someone says his name. So. If you wrote a poem about me, I'd never die, would I? And if it was good enough, then neither would you –

HER. Is that all you care about, your legacy?

HIM. No – What – No, just –

HER. Me immortalising you.

HIM. It was just a thought –

HER. I slept with someone.

That night. When I told you I was out walking. He was still in my mouth. I wanted to keep him there for as long as possible. I met him, in a bar. I went out walking, and I saw this bar, I just wanted to go and sit in there. Just sit in the dark, not even drink. Just sit, listen. And I did, I was just sitting there. When this man came up to me, older man, and he had all this cash, he could actually buy me a drink. I forgot how nice that was, to be bought a drink by a man in a bar. And he kept saying one more. One more, one more, and I kept saying okay, because that's what I do, really, the real me, the me I really like. And before I knew it we were in his hotel room. Little hotel, shabby little place really, fan didn't work. But he had a river in his suitcase, a whole river, I could have swum for days in that room, and no – before you ask – I didn't think about you. I didn't carry you, you weren't stood in the corner, I didn't think of you when it was happening, or after it was done, I was totally myself, and it felt fucking extraordinary.

Pause.

HIM. Is this real. Did this really happen.

HER. Yes, it happened.

HIM. It's not a lie.

HER. No… So. I suppose you want to leave now.

HIM. Not really.

HER. Why not?

HIM. Because I love you. You made a mistake. You hurt me, but I love you –

HER. Well I don't love you, I can't, can I, if I did that –

HIM. People do that and still love people.

HER. Why are you doing this to yourself?

I think you should go. For real this time, I'm done, I'm fucking / done with it –

HIM. I'm doing this because I think you love me too. Deep down. I do, I think you love me –

HER. I don't, I don't, so fucking go. Get out. Get out of my life, you fucking –

She hits him, over and over, until he grabs her – her throat – reactionary, self-defence maybe, but a line crossed. She holds his hand there. She squeezes his hand tighter. She looks at him for a second. He lets go, ashamed.

In the dark, he thrashes, reeling in pain.

He is painting – creating something horrific.

They stare at each other for ages. It's almost like a staring contest. Who'll smile first. Years.

HIM. I don't think we've been introduced.

HER. I'll have a wine, thank you.

HIM. Oh, uh –

HER. Red wine, and be quick about it, thank you –

HIM. Oh, no, uh – This is awkward – I'm actually – I'm actually the artist. I'm the painter. Of these.

HER. No, you're not.

HIM. I am, yeah.

HER. I thought you were a waiter. You look like a waiter.

HIM. Yeah, no.

HER. You painted these? *You?*

HIM. Yeah, yeah. These ones, here, these two walls… The others are… someone else…

HER. Well well…

   Beat.

HIM. Are you a collector, or…

HER. Oh yes, I collect, yes, I have a vast collection. My manor's full of them.

HIM. Your manor?

HER. Yes. Oh, how rude of me, I apologise… I'm Lady… Lady Fanny… Something funny?

HIM. Lady-fanny?

HER. Enchanté.

HIM. How did you hear about the showing?

HER. Oh, I saw your face in a magazine. Art magazine, and I thought, I know that face. Which isn't always a given, but I did, I knew it, and I got so giddy all of a sudden, I was just so incredibly. Proud. My chest hurt, looking at that photo.

Beat.

HIM. You've been off the map for a while.

HER. Yes, yes, right off it. Fell right off the face of the earth for a bit there.

HIM. People were worried about you. Thought you might have died, even.

HER. How dare they. I descend from a long line of survivors. If they knew me at all, they'd know that.

HIM. Well, they looked for you. All over. All your haunts. Your flat.

HER. Ah yes, the old estate. Terribly sad business, but the offer was just too good. Moved to the manor, yes. South, if you'd believe it. South of the river. Overrun with foxes. More foxes than people.

HIM. South.

HER. Very far south, yes. I hardly ever ventured north again. For fear of… old ghosts…

HIM. Well. I wish you'd told people. Could have saved a few years of worry.

HER. Not years.

HIM. No. Years.

Beat.

HER. Yes, well, I couldn't communicate with the outside world
you see, not for a long while. I was struck down with a rare
affliction – exotic actually, almost entirely unheard of. I'd
taken to river swimming, you see. Every morning I'd hop in
the river and swim for hours at a time – upstream,
downstream... but I was noticing I was gaining weight. It
was the strangest thing: the more I swam, the heavier I
became, I was getting bigger and bigger. Turns out I hadn't
been closing my mouth. I'd been taking in all that river water
for months and months and months, and so there I was, with
this giant belly, pregnant with a whole river, until eventually
I sprung a leak, out of my bum, and someone had to plug me
up with corks. Roll me into the hospital – a giant wobbly ball
of a woman. They drained me. It took months and months, a
year, maybe I don't know, but it was awful. I loved having
the river in me. But they told me it was bad for me. They
squeezed me dry, a vat at a time, and let me go... Problem is.
It's not like it's just done now. I'd gotten so used to it. My
body had stretched. And now I feel all. Saggy. Empty. All
this space to fill up again... And I so missed the art world.
I've missed looking at it. Quite terribly. I forgot how
beautiful it was... I don't suppose you'd like to go
somewhere. And. Fill me in. Not like that. Cheeky –

HIM. I – I'm with someone. I'm... I'm sober. I should have
said straight away – I've been sober for a while now. She's
only known me sober, actually. Sorry.

HER. What are you saying sorry for? That's. Wonderful –
That's great. *Sober.* Good, and you're happy? 'And you're
happy', of course you're happy –

HIM. I wasn't. For a long time, I really... I really wasn't.

HER. When you painted these?

HIM. What?

HER. When you painted these. Were you happy?

HIM. No.

HER. Well then. You're welcome. I should take commission…

You've immortalised me. Sort of. Or the other way around.
Ha –

HIM. Anything you like, in particular?

HER. Well, the one over there. The main one. Sort of spider-
person thing… It's the strangest thing, I found myself crying,
looking at that one. Inexplicably, just burst out of me.
Someone came over to check. I said it was the price, I mean
eye-watering. I saw someone had bought it.

HIM. Yeah. Yes. It's an old one.

You've seen it before, actually. The night we met.

HER. Oh?

HIM. You never remembered that night.

HER. No, I did, I do. Something about… a window, a scar?

HIM. My arm.

HER. See? I do remember.

HIM. Or you remember me telling you about it.

HER. Well, that's the same thing really, isn't it? All just…
Stories… really… Were you this fantastic to look at before?
I don't think you were. Your skin is so –

HIM. It's what being a boring sober bastard will do for you. Not
yellow any more. Did you know I was yellow? There are
some good places now, you know. Pills. And I hate pills.

HER. Hospitals, I remember.

HIM. But these are good. I could help you find the one that
works for you –

HER. What, you'd be my doctor would you?

HIM. Of course, yeah... Well, no, actually. It's – Has to be – Cos we've... had... You know... Relations...

HER. Relations.

HIM. Shut up –

HER. Because you know me, *biblically* –

HIM. Just the rules –

HER. So grown up, aren't you. All of a sudden. Such an expert now you've returned from the great dry desert. Teach me, oh learnèd one –

HIM. Alright, anyway, I should – I should probably go mingle –

HER. Yes, no, absolutely, go mingle, go mingle with your dingle –

HIM. Thank you for coming.

HER. You're welcome. And good luck with everything. This. Her.

HIM. Thanks.

HER. Another life, maybe. Past life. Ha ha... You know, I might stay and mingle too, actually. I love schmoozing with artists and their schmoozy little circles – I always have. The stories we tell each other...

Pause.

HIM. We could get a coffee. If you wanted – I could get us a – If you gave me an hour –

What – What's this look now –

HER. Total agogness. I'm totally agog. You're buying me a drink.

HIM. Fuck off –

HER. This is what agog looks like –

HIM. Just a coffee, that's all. Or tea. Tea's safe, isn't it? No one's exploded over a cup of tea.

HER. Would I have to drink tea?

HIM. No.

HER. Your new poison.

HIM. Mm-hm.

HER. Of all the poisons you could choose in this world.
     Lapsang souchong.

HIM. It's nice.

HER. You can't like that.

HIM. I do, actually –

HER. Really?

HIM. Well, no, not really. But I don't think I ever really knew
     what I liked… And it's nice to be told what do to,
     sometimes. Drink this. Eat this. Taken care of. Nice to know
     someone wants you to stay in the world, even if you don't.

HER. You don't want to stay in the world?

   Beat.

HIM. uh, no, yeah –

HER. Jesus –

HIM. What? I said yeah –

HER. After like five minutes –

HIM. I want to stay in the world, yes, right now I do.

   Beat.

HER. Sure you don't mind me having this in front of you?

HIM. No, no. Enjoy it. Please.

   Beat.

HER. I can't believe this, can you?

HIM. What?

HER. That I'm here with you, now. You're really real. I can actually touch yo–

He flinches a little, pulls away.

HIM. Sorry, just…

HER. No, no…

Pause.

You smell the same.

HIM. Uh-huh.

HER. Even from here. Do I?

You won't explode.

He leans a little, smells her, nods.

Funny, isn't it. How smells go deeper. And songs, I find. Like the other day. I heard this song. I was walking, and I heard this song, and I had this image, suddenly, this image floated in front of me, of us, singing together.

HIM. What?

HER. Yes. Me and you. Singing together.

HIM. I don't think I ever sang with you. That won't have been me.

HER. Well whoever it was I remember thinking it was very sexy, I remember thinking I wanted to shag them rotten for it.

HIM. Then it was me, yeah, that's right.

HER. Does she know you're with me?

HIM. Uh, what? Uh. No.

HER. Was she there? Earlier.

HIM. Yes. Yeah. I'm not telling you which one –

HER. Does she know who I am?

HIM. I don't – Uh. I don't think so.

HER. You've never spoken about me?

HIM. (No.)

HER. Not with her, anyway.

HIM. Not with anyone.

HER. Hm. So, it's like I never existed at all. In your (stratosphere).

HIM. How's the drink?

HER. You want a sip?

HIM. No.

HER. Then why are you asking?

HIM. Being polite –

HER. You want me to describe how it feels?

HIM. No –

HER. You ever wank over me?

HIM. Wha– Fuck –

He coughs up tea.

HER. Jesus – I mean, we're sat here, we're sat talking like you've never kissed my neck, like you don't know me at all –

HIM. Well, I mean, I don't, really.

HER. Yes you do. You know me.

HIM. I know a handful of things, from a million years ago. I know things you *allowed* me to know, that's all –

HER. You told me you loved me, once. You said you carried me. You remember that?

You still carry me? Or did you drop me, somewhere along the line?

Beat.

HIM. Can we just – Please, can we just sit here and act like
    we're two old friends having a drink.

HER. Drinking buddies, you mean? Sure. Sure. We can do
    that –

HIM. Are you working at the moment?

HER. Yes, I'm a serial killer.

HIM. Okay –

HER. I collect men's body parts. Teeth, spit –

HIM. I guess I... I had an image, in my head, that one day
    you'd start – You know I always hoped you'd write again.
    Maybe in that book I got you.

HER. Book? I don't remember a book...

HIM. Course.

HER. I haven't written anything in a long time. I don't have
    a muse like you.

HIM. You're not with anyone in particular?

HER. No one in particular, no. I have two rules: stay single and
    drink doubles.

HIM. Don't you get lonely?

HER. Oh no. There are always people, darling. That's the thing
    with this pursuit, there are always bodies to lie beside. Sit
    with at a bar. But not one in particular stands out. They all
    sort of merge, really. They're all just one big homogeneous
    blob of a man – hair, skin – all of them –

HIM. All of them?

HER. Don't think you're special or anything, you get lost in the
    mix too. I do it all the time. Could be you, there, in one story,
    could be someone else. Could be someone I met last week,
    ten years ago, I don't know, really... All one blob... I
    suppose here's where you tell me that your lady friend is
    completely unique, a rare orchid –

HIM. No. She's better than that. She's normal. She's safe. She gives me structure.

HER. Jesus. I don't know what I'd do if someone described me as that –

HIM. Oh, I don't think there's any danger.

HER. Like scaffolding. She's shaped you into what I see before me.

HIM. She helped, yes.

HER. Don't you think that's sad? That she'll never get to see the real you.

HIM. Real me?

HER. The you I knew.

HIM. You think that was the real me? Why? Because – Because I was in pain most of the time?

HER. Like a real artist.

HIM. That's not the real me. That's just the me with you, the me you remember – Talk about shaping someone –

HER. Maybe that's the most authentic you there is. Most alive anyway. But instead this poor safe cow has to make do with this nine-to-five, honey-I'm-home, comb-over –

HIM. Okay –

HER. Why are you looking at me like that?

HIM. Just. Recognition is all.

HER. What the fuck does that mean?

HIM. It means, yes, I carry you. Of course I carry you. But mostly I think about the good bits. I try to forget all this stuff.

HER. What stuff?

HIM. Is this why you found me? Cos this isn't my job, you know, I'm not some keeper of your fucking story, I don't remember most / of it either –

HER. You said it, you said *this stuff*, what's *this stuff*?

HIM. You trying to hurt me. To get a rise out of me – or push me away when it got too close, because, because maybe that's what you think passion is. You going missing for weeks, and then taking me to your dad's funeral, and telling me we're drinking buddies, and pretending that you slept with someone –

HER. So, you want me to apologise then, for hurting you? Because we weren't married you know –

HIM. Yes. I fucking do –

HER. I'm sorry for hurting you.

HIM. Thank you –

HER. Now do you want to apologise to me?

HIM. For what?

HER. For using me to hurt you.

HIM. Jesus –

HER. Why else would you have stuck around? If it was so terrible, if I did all those terrible things. Maybe it's because it made your art better? It made you a more interesting person? A doomed artist, that's using me –

HIM. I stuck around because I… (loved you.)

(I loved you so much. And I was sure you loved me too.)

Pause.

HER. What are the good bits?

HIM. What?

HER. What, you can tell me all the terrible things I did, and none of the good?

HIM. Well, what about me? I mean, I'm lost in some fucking blob of men, apparently. You can't tell me anything about me –

HER. I remember your smell.

HIM. Right now you can –

HER. And that you're a magnificent kisser. I remember that. And you used to say 'get ready' sometimes. When we were having sex. 'Get ready.'

HIM. Did I?

HER. I pulled your tooth out once. In my kitchen. You made us steal wine from a church. We cleared the flat of bottles. And we sang.

HIM. These aren't things about *me*, these are anecdotes – These are about you, really – That's / classic narcissism.

HER. No they're not – I'm not a fucking narcissist.

HIM. What do you remember about my life?

Anything?

HER. You were sick as a child.

HIM. What happened when I got better? To my mum and dad? What did my mum say to me? I told you this. Like it would have been easier if I… Fucking hell –

HER. I'm sorry –

HIM. This was big stuff, this was big fucking stuff I told you about –

HER. It doesn't mean I don't care.

HIM. Yes, it does. Remembering is a choice, sometimes –

HER. Not with me, not with my brain.

HIM. Well then that's worse, then, that's scary, you should be scared, cos that fucking terrifies me. That's the main reason I wanted to stop. As well as the sickness, it was cos I was terrified of that. Of looking back and just… fucking nothing there. Years and years, just (gone) … I got sober so I could keep – So I could *reclaim* the little I remember of my life. And yes, a part of that is you. Quite a big part, actually. I got sober so I could have you somewhere. If not all of you, if not for real, then…

Sorry, I'm – uh... I shouldn't have – It's stirring up a lot of things, / seeing –

HER. You can have me now if you want.

Right now. You can have me.

Pause.

She reaches out, and touches his head. The back of his head.

Do you feel that? When she touches you.

Not quite –

HIM. You need to stop –

HER. Okay. You want me to stop? I can stop. Watch this. You see this? My last sip ever. You watch, watch me – Why are you smiling?

HIM. This has happened before –

HER. Well I mean it this time, I do, this time I really mean it...

HIM. And then what? I'm supposed to just – What? Go back with you, to your new place, forget everything I've been doing, forget my new life, *leave her.*

HER. Yes. If that's what you want.

Really want, the real you.

You can have me, and I can have you. If that's what you want. Right now...

They begin to have sex.

Tell me.

HIM. We'll start with... diazepam. For anxiety, withdrawal...

HER. uh-huh...

HIM. Some Librium.

HER. Mmm.

HIM. Thiamine, vitamin B.

HER. Fuck yeah.

HIM. Synapses mend. The brain starts to heal itself – memories come back.

HER. Yes.

HIM. Pabrinex, which is a shot in the arse. A nurse comes to do it.

HER. A nurse.

HIM. Vitamin C. Or I could just stick a lime up your bum.

HER. Yes please.

HIM. Oranges, peppers, strawberries, I'll shove them all up your arse. Pears. Plums, chestnuts, blueberries, broccoli – Clean you up from inside.

HER. Deep clean.

HIM. Turmeric, ginger, dark chocolate, raw garlic.

HER. Deeper –

HIM. You'll have light in your eyes. Your lips. Your tongue – We'll do it every day. Over and over. And we'll get you clean.

HER. You'll clean me.

HIM. I'll clean you –

HER. Clean me out –

HIM. Fuck. Fuck –

HER. Fuck –

HIM. Fuck this fucking country –

HER. What? Whoa / what's happened?

HIM. They said – That bitch just told me – You / know the one at the clinic –

HER. Stop – hang on – You're shaking –

HIM. She's always judged me, I told you, she's always looked at me like I was – This is the problem, the basic underlying problem of everything, is fucking *empathy*. No one gives a shit any more, do they, about anyone else, and I begged her. I actually – Literally, I got on my knees in the reception –

HER. You're racing, I don't know what / you're talking about –

HIM. I was actually crying, on my knees, saying please, please, we need them. We really need them. They're working. They're working, aren't they working?

HER. Can you just please tell me what's going?

HIM. They're stopping the pills. She said we're not a priority any more. I mean, when were we ever a fucking priority? We're pariahs, aren't we. 'Their own fault, fuck them, let them rot. Good riddance.' This fucking country spends millions getting us to drink, and then when we start dying from it, all they say is hurry up. The pills were working.

HER. I know.

HIM. They were really working. Things were working.

HER. We can work something out –

HIM. Oh yeah, like fucking what?

HER. I don't know – Don't talk to me / like that –

HIM. Expert here all of a sudden –

HER. Don't need those pills to medicate me.

HIM. What do you mean?

HER. I mean… You can go out and buy some medicine. Little bottle of something to medicate me with…

HIM. You – You want me to get a bottle of –

HER. If you think I still need it…

HIM. That's not – I don't think that's a good idea –

HER. It's you who was so worked up –

HIM. Yes, because one in twenty die trying cold turkey, right –

HER. What?

HIM. And having a bottle in here. In the flat. That just feels like – That feels like a hand grenade lying about –

HER. You can hide it if you don't trust me –

HIM. I – No, it's not – I – I trust you –

HER. And I trust you. Can you trust yourself with it?

HIM. Of course. Yes. I'm fine –

HER. So...? It's medicine. Isn't it... We think of it like that.

HIM. Just medicine. Just for a few more weeks.

HER. Yeah.

What are you doing?

HIM. I thought. A spoon – A teaspoon – Keep it, you know. Medicinal. Like you said.

HER. Right – okay, spoon-fed –

HIM. I watered it down. I used a pipette. You / should barely taste it –

HER. Where did you get a pipette from?

HIM. God, I'm shaking a bit –

HER. Are you nervous?

HIM. I don't know, yeah, I think so.

HER. What? That I'll be like a shark? Drop of blood in water. My eyes will go black.

HIM. No, no, just... It's been good. Hasn't it. This bit.

HER. Keeping me, you mean. Being in charge.

HIM. N-no, no, I mean –

HER. It's been good, yeah. It's good.

I'll be fine –

HIM. Yeah, I know, okay, okay… Ready?

HER. Yes, doctor.

HIM. Okay… Miss…

HER. I like that.

HIM. What?

HER. Sexy. Sexy doctor.

HIM. Ahem.

HER. I'm an old beauty. Dying. Tragic. We're in Pamplona. Summer. Stifling hot. Fiesta. An old hotel room. Chiffon curtains. Iron bed. Outside the bulls are running in the street. This medicine is my last chance.

HIM. Okay –

HER. It's so hot, doctor. I'm sweating –

HIM. Well, let's save your life, shall we…

HER. I hope so… For I see now… how beautiful the world is…

HIM. Yes. Now. Open up…

God blows through the room

How was that then? Miss…

HER. Uh. Fine.

HIM. Oh, what's happened to our dame?

HER. It was fine.

HIM. Was it strong?

HER. Uh, no, no.

HIM. Could you taste it?

HER. The pipette worked.

HIM. Yeah, yeah, I'm proud of that –

HER. I just – I just have one a day, do I?

HIM. Unless you feel really ill.

HER. Okay. Okay. Okay –

HIM. We'll do this dance once a day for the next couple of weeks. Before you know it…

HER. I didn't hear you.

HIM. What?

HER. Come in. I've got something for you. Surprise.

HIM. What – What is it?

Her poetry book.

Is this… This is the one I got you?

HER.…First couple of pages…

He opens it. He smiles. He reads. He takes his time, looks at her, reads it again. He cries. He smiles. She smiles. She stops smiling.

Is this the same? As it was. Are we?

I can't remember.

I don't think we are.

I can't remember.

HIM. Why don't we do something? Why don't we go out tonight? For a meal maybe, a sing-song somewhere. Remember that – Doing that?

HER. A sing-song?

HIM. Yeah.

HER. Sober?

HIM. Yes.

HER. A sober sing-song –

HIM. We can sing without it. Come on. We're fun, aren't we.
I'm fun. You think I'm fun.

HER. Uh…

HIM. Fuck off, I'm fun. We don't need a drink to have –

HER. I just need a second –

HIM. Okay.

HER. Lots of people in there.

HIM. You're not going to explode, okay. I'll hold your hand.
We'll just pretend – If you like, just pretend. You know? Act
like it's the old days.

HER. What?

HIM. You know. My round…

On me. I insist. Pretty lady.

HER. Pretty lady.

HIM. You come here often? I've not seen you around.

HER. I don't think this is –

HIM. This is the centre of an ancient triangle. People go
missing here. Start again… Aren't – You're that poet, aren't
you? That famous poet?

HER. No.

HIM. You are, I love your stuff. Do that one for me. That one
that's about arms and biting and blood –

HER. Don't –

HIM. I'm a singer.

HER. Are you.

HIM. Don't you find that sexy or something?

HER. No.

HIM. You haven't heard me sing yet…

HER. You've got to be kidding me…

HIM. Not even a bit –

HER. I'm not doing this –

HIM. We love this one.

HER. Do we love this one? I don't love this one –

HIM. I'm sure we do. This song. This is the song we sang. Our song.

HER. Our song.

HIM. Come on…

He sings karaoke.

Okay this bit is both of us. Both of us, come on.

After a while, she joins him.

For a while they're good together. It's forced fun. She becomes aware of herself. Of other people, watching. She stops. She watches him. She doesn't feel anything. He looks at her. He knows. A while.

HER. I didn't hear you.

HIM. What?

HER. Come in. Say you're home.

HIM. Do I need to say I'm home when I'm home?

HER. Yes.

HIM. Why?

HER. Just something people shout, isn't it, when they come through the door, normal people.

HIM. Why, so your bloke has a chance to hide in the cupboard?

HER. Yes, exactly that, so he knows to hurry up and finish.

HIM. You want me to pretend I'm in a sitcom or / something –

HER. Exactly that, yes please.

HIM. You want me to shout honey I'm home.

HER. That's exactly what I want, why do you have to pick / at everything –

HIM. HONEY I'M HOME.

Beat.

HER. Well don't stop there, I was enjoying that.

HIM. I'm exhausted.

HER. Long day?

HIM. They're all long.

HER. I thought you were nearly done with this hotel piece?

HIM. What are you doing?

HER. I'm asking you questions about your day, this is what people do –

HIM. She wants to know about my day –

HER. Yes, she does, 'she', when did I become 'she' –

HIM. I haven't been working on the hotel piece. I've been trying to paint something for us. For you. Another version of the old painting. The one I sold. From my art college –

HER. The… spider-person thing –

HIM. I had a few sketches to go from, but it's mainly memory. So of course it's shit. It's fucking shit, it's nothing, and I've tried, over and over, but it's just nothing. It's because I'm happy. I'm so *happy* now. So I left the studio, this morning, and I walked, and I went and stood outside a pub. A pub we used to go to – I stood outside, thinking about going in, just have one, maybe, kept crossing the road, looking in, crossing back, fuck it, just one, see if it does anything, see if it stirs anything up. See if I can get that back. And then this old bloke came dribbling over to me, came spitting and dribbling, asking for money and then he stopped and looked at me… and asked how you were doing. Said your name, out loud, said what a great girl you were, great girl, he said, great girl, and for a second, I saw you, there, inside, Friday money clutched in your hand, 'next one's on me', some story, some character, everyone laughing, hoarse, coughing, and me, watching you, and just. Loving you, like that, more than anything, more than ever, like that… And then I left. I gave the old fella a couple of quid, said have one for us, and then I came home… How was your day?

HER. Oh, fine.

HIM. Good.

HER. I went for a nice walk.

HIM. Oh.

HER. To the park. I went for a nice walk around the park, the flowers, and squirrels and children playing, mothers, my age I think, I don't know, they look like actors on a set, I walked around this film set, and then I walked to the butcher's, and got a chicken, and I came home, and I cleaned, and I got ready for you.

HIM. And that was your day.

HER. That was my day.

HIM. Good –

HER. Oh, and I found a bottle.

We must have missed it, somehow, when we did the clean-out. Little bottle. Half drunk. Behind the towels... I thought we checked there, but maybe we didn't. Must have missed it. Do you think? Because. I could swear we checked there. But we all know what my memory's like. You're the keeper of all that... Anyway, I threw it away. I tipped it away. In one go. Are you proud of me?

HIM. I'm proud of you.

HER. Thank you, that means something... We both had a test today then. Both passed.

HIM. Yes...

HER. You haven't said anything about my outfit.

HIM. Oh.

HER. The coat.

HIM. That's my coat.

HER. Yeah. I saw it the other day and thought, that looks like a flasher's coat. The tan. I thought, that's what flashers wear, when they flash people. So.

HIM. So?

HER. Ta-dah.

What d'you think?

You know, it's been a while...

HIM. We've been busy –

HER. I haven't. I haven't been busy –

HIM. I'm just – You know, I've just come in and the studio was –

HER. Why don't you just touch me. Why don't we start there. My fucking shoulder, or something, you won't explode.

I'll touch you then.

What about this? If I put my hand there. When I put my hand through your hair… It's nearly the same. Isn't it. Nearly.

I didn't throw it out. The bottle.

That woman. One you saw today. One you dreamt about. One you're in love with. I want her back too… So… Cheers.

HIM. Cheers.

God blows through the room

Oh fuck.

HER. What?

HIM. I've pissed myself.

HER. Jesus, you haven't –

HIM (*laughing*). I have, yeah. Fuck. Sorry. Fuck –

HER. Come and sit down –

HIM. It's good here, isn't it. You don't get looks out here. First thing in the morning. You noticed that? No one's looking at us. It's the bus stop that does it. Looks like we're just waiting for the bus, doesn't it. We're just normal people waiting for our bus, we're one of them, going to work or to the shops or the vet's. Don't you think?

HER. Sure.

HIM. So you don't then?

HER. I just said sure –

HIM. After five fucking / minutes –

HER. Please don't start with me / they'll open up in a minute –

HIM. Look at me. Look at me and tell me – I won't kick off. I promise – Pretend you don't know me. Like we never met – what's that?

HER (*smiling*). What?

HIM. That fucking grin, there?

HER. We've done this before.

HIM. What?

HER. We pretended to be strangers before, you / remember –

HIM. Just fucking do it will you –

HER. You come here often?

HIM. What?

HER. This. Bus stop. You catch many buses / from here –

HIM. No, don't fucking – I didn't say talk to me, I said look at me, just look at me and tell / me what you –

HER. You look like you're waiting / for a bus.

HIM. You didn't look for long enough –

HER. Oh my God –

HIM. FUCK'S SAKE, WHY ARE YOU ALWAYS LAUGHING AT ME.

Beat.

HER. Here's what I see, you fucking maniac, I see a man standing by a bus stop, early morning, thus he must be waiting for a bus –

HIM. Do it again –

HER. This is so / fucking stupid –

HIM. Please. Just. Once. Properly. Properly look. Please.

What do I look like?

Tell me.

HER. You look like you're about to fall apart. Like you're about to vanish, you're so thin. Your skin looks like wet Rizla, there's blue underneath, like a bruise, like you're bleeding somewhere, and you stink, of rot, of sour, your organs are eating themselves, you're full of acid, and it's wasting you from the inside out, in front of my eyes, you're wasting, and it's terrible. It's terrible. Because if you look like that, then so do I.

HIM. I finished it.

HER. What?

HIM. The painting. Our painting. The limbs.

HER. Already? Wait – Wait –

HIM. What do you think?

Think it's like it was before? Remember. Gallery. My studio…?

HER. What are you… Get up. What are you doing?

HIM. Will you marry me.

HER.… What?

HIM. Will you –

HER. You're preposterous, this is insane –

HIM. Do you love me?

Because I love you. Very much. In the whole world, you're the only thing I love, and I've told you that, so many times, but I can't remember you saying it back. Have you ever said it back to me?

Do you love me?

HER. I don't think you love me, really, I think you just love the way I make / you feel –

HIM. I need you to answer me. I need you to say it right now.

HER. Why?

HIM. Because I'm sick. I'm so sick. I need you to love me,
that's what I need, I need you to say that, and you'll save me.

HER. I might love you. I might do.

Or maybe I'm just drunk.

He thrashes in the dark. He starts to tear the painting apart.

HIM. Take it. Take it. Take it, please / take it.

HER. That's blood, you're bleeding –

HIM. My hair. Here. Anything. Take my hair –

HER. Hello, / ambulance –

HIM. Take my eye lashes. Take my skin. Please. / Take
everything. Take my body –

HER. It's my partner, he's – / He's hurting himself in our –

HIM. Tear it off. Tear it all fucking...

*He tears his clothes off. He tears his skin off. He tears his
painting to pieces. It's a nightmare.*

HIM *in a neck brace.* HER *stood there, holding dead
flowers.*

A long time. Who'll cry first.

S-staring.

HER. Sorry. Yes. Sorry.

HIM. Wh-what   t-time i-is it?

HER. Late. Early. I don't know.

Beat.

HIM. Wh-what are th-those?

HER. Flowers.

HIM. D-dead.

HER. Yeah, well –

HIM. '*O-our dearest… Gemima. F-forever… i-in our hearts.*'

HER. Ah…

HIM. You s-stole these?

HER. No. Yes –

HIM. F-fuck –

HER. I didn't – I didn't realise there was a. Card. That's funny – Got to admit, that's funny. Gemima. Sorry.

Do you remember what happened?

HIM. N-not r-really. A w-window?

HER. Yes.

HIM. G-glass. Th-then. B-black.

HER. Mm. It's okay, I won't remember either, soon enough…

Beat.

HIM. G-got s-something for y-you too.

HER. Oh?

He hands her a tooth. It's real.

It's…

HIM. M-my t-tooth. C-came out. C-can keep it.

HER. Thank you.

She puts it in her pocket.

I stopped by the church on the way here. Thought I'd stock up.

HIM. Wh-what?

HER. Wine.

When we broke in?

Beat.

Time to resurrect you. Don't you think?

Beat.

HIM. D-did you kn-know I w-was y-yellow? Wh-when I c-came in. B-bright y-yellow.

HER. No.

HIM. M-my liver.

HER. Okay. Well, livers regenerate, so –

HIM. N-not this one. H-hand g-grenade. L-like you s-said. L-luck of the draw.

Beat.

HER. Is this real? Is this real or –

HIM. V-very real. I-I've got s-six months. If I don't s-stop now. E-even one d-drink. O-one m-more s-sip.

HER. Not a sip, they always say a sip, I mean a *sip*.

HIM. A s-sip. Y-yeah. S-so. Th-this is it.

Goodbye –

HER. No it's not, shut up –

HIM. Wh-what?

HER. Shut up, I don't do goodbyes, if you knew me at all, you'd know I don't do that –

HIM. B-but –

HER. I don't care, I don't want that, no, there's more time. Isn't there. If we try. Together.

HIM. Y-you s-said this before.

HER. Well, I mean it this time. I really mean it, let's do it. Forget the wine, I'll – I'll pour it away –

HIM. And th-then what?

HER. And, then. We get you out of here. You always hated hospitals. Let's go home.

HIM. H-home?

HER. My home. Ours. How does that sound? We can sneak you out – Don't look suspicious, we're just popping out for a breath of fresh –

Thank fuck for that, eh?

Just up here.

Here.

HIM. Wh-when's the n-nurse coming?

HER. Not till next week now. They had to cut it back, remember?

HIM. O-oh.

HER. I think we've got a pill stashed somewhere. You want a pill? A diazapem or –

HIM. N-no i-it's okay. Th-the nurse c-can d-do it wh-when she comes.

HER. What?

HIM. Wh-what t-time is sh-she coming?

HER. She's not coming till next week.

HIM. Oh.

HER. I just told you.

HIM. Oh.

HER. Let me go look for a pill, I've got one, I'm –

HIM. Fuck, fuck –

HER. What's –

HIM. Th-they're e-everywhere –

HER. What?

HIM. S-spiders –

HER. Oh, darling, you're just – you're dreaming –

HIM. A-all o-over me – m-my skin –

HER. Come here –

HIM. My s-skin's coming off, l-look – M-my teeth –

HER. You're just having a nightmare, / darling –

HIM. A-am I h-here? A-am I d-dead?

HER. Just, just hang on – Hold my hand –

HIM. I-I'm dead / I-I'm d-dead –

HER. Hang on, hang on – Hello, yes, we need some help please, my partner, he's… We need someone to come… We don't have anything here. We don't have any pills, we don't have anything –

HIM. I need you to do it.

HER What?

HIM. M-medicine.

Beat.

HER. I'm not doing that, darling.

HIM. J-just a s-sip. S-save my life a-again –

HER. You can't even have a sip, darling –

HIM. I'm s-scared –

HER. This is going too quick, we're not / here yet –

HIM. I'm s-scared, p-please, I n-need it, please.

HER. It has to be the tiniest sip –

HIM. O-okay. O-okay.

HER. Just to help you sleep, just a tiny bit, that's it.

    I couldn't find your pipette. You remember that? We had a pipette?

HIM. You don't have to be scared.

HER. I'm not –

HIM. I'll be alright.

HER. I know.

    Beat.

HIM. Y-you c-come h-here often?

HER. What?

HIM. N-not s-seen y-you around...

HER. Oh...

    No, I'm... I'm new...

HIM. Y-you're s-so beautiful.

    My r-round.

HER. Oh, I don't actually drink any more –

HIM. B-bullshit. L-let m-me b-buy y-you a drink. I'm very
r-rich, y-you s-see. F-famous a-artist.

J-just one. Last o-one ever...

HER. Actually, we can't – I'm not doing this, we can't do this –

HIM. Wh-what?

HER. This, this is too dangerous, even a sip, they said, so –
So, I'm going to pour it away. You can watch, watch me, I'm
going to pour it all away...

Pause.

HIM. It's the only way you love me.

A long time.

So.

Cheers.

*Lights. Sobering. A church hall. A wet day. Probably
a Tuesday. The middle of the afternoon.*

*An AA meeting. Maybe a circle of chairs. Maybe a few
people, even, coming in from the cold, getting teas and
coffees, talking quietly, taking their seats.*

She is stood at the coffee urn, looking at HIM. *She is upset.*

He nods, smiles at her. Then he's gone.

HER. Uh.

Hi.

Uh... I'm. Alice... and I'm an alcoholic...

(*Hi Alice.*)

Hi… Uh… I… I came to one of these. A million years ago. And I met someone. At the coffee, thing, urn, vat. Charlie. His name.

And anyway, he turned out to be the love of my life…

And this morning I buried him.

I just came from the, uh… I didn't know anyone there. And no one knew me. So, I figured this was the place to come, seeing as I was – Seeing as no one knows me anyway, now.

She has her poetry book.

And I've been. Sitting here, trying to – Trying to think about him, and about what I might say, about him, about *us*, but I only have these bits. These little bits of him, and I'm not even sure some of those are even real, even him. And most of them are awful, I was really awful, sometimes.

But I still wish I had more. I just… I wish I had more.

I want to get him back. Somewhere. Keep him alive *somewhere*… Honour him.

He's there again.

They stare at each other for a long time. Like a staring contest. Who'll smile first. Years.

CHARLIE. I cut my arm.

ALICE. Did you?

CHARLIE. On the window, look, I'll have a scar there.

ALICE. Something to remember me by. Which is yours?

CHARLIE. This one.

ALICE. Right.

CHARLIE. What do you think?

ALICE. Very. Black.

CHARLIE. Yeah. Yeah, you know what, this was a bad idea, let's go –

ALICE. No, stop that, fuck off, I'm just – I'm just working it out –

CHARLIE. You don't need to work it – It should just be a feeling thing –

ALICE. What's this thing in the middle here?

CHARLIE. It's a person.

ALICE. No, this thing in the middle –

CHARLIE. Yeah that's a person.

ALICE. You ever met a person before? It's got eight limbs.

CHARLIE. And two heads, yeah.

ALICE. Right, so what sort of person's that?

CHARLIE. The first person… First person ever created looked like that.

ALICE. Did it?

CHARLIE. It's just a story I like –

ALICE. About the first person.

CHARLIE. First people yeah.

ALICE. Who were born with eight limbs.

CHARLIE. And two heads, yes.

ALICE. Two heads.

CHARLIE. And two genitalia.

ALICE. Double dicks.

CHARLIE. Or fannies, yeah / or both.

ALICE. Couple of fannies, why not both –

CHARLIE. The children of the moon, they were called. Big ball
of limbs. They spent their days rolling around the earth.
Happy. Wanting for nothing. But the gods didn't like that, so
they sent down a lightning bolt, which split them all in two.
One head, two arms, two legs. And they were scattered
across the planet. All these half-people, flung far away from
themselves. Which was cruel. But not the cruellest thing the
gods did. The cruellest thing was leaving them all with a
memory. Dark and watery – a memory of themselves
complete. Full and wanting nothing. And that was their
curse, forever. All of mankind, to forever half-remember the
other half. To want, and spend the rest of our days wanting...
to be full again...

HER. And you think this will be the one?

HIM. One, what?

HER. That you'll be remembered for.

HIM. I don't know.

I hope so.

*She looks at him for a long time. She tries to remember him.
They kiss.*

God blows through the room

We see it all. All of them, over and over, on repeat

Blackout.

www.nickhernbooks.co.uk

facebook.com/nickhernbooks

twitter.com/nickhernbooks